# Chapter 1: Introduction to Gi

This chapter gives you some basic information about Gimp.

## Features

Gimp has an extensive feature set. Below is a list of the most commonly known ones:

- resize / scale images
- convert images between file formats
- retouch images using filters
- add new content to images using layers
- draw / edit along paths

Gimp is extensible through plugins. Plugins are used to add advanced features such as creating animated GIFs.

## Pitfalls

What makes Gimp hard to learn?

Not everybody chooses to work with computers. For them it's not about passion, it's only a simple tool they use to get things done. To make matters worse, Gimp looks, works and behaves differently from some of the everyday computer programs.

This can cause disappointment and in some cases users turn away from the program.

I believe everyone should get the chance to be instructed properly on how to use Gimp.

What are the concepts to be learnt throughout this book?

## Layers

Gimp creates images that are made up of layers. Layers should be thought of as building blocks. This powerful feature allows the user to go back to their work later and finetune the layers independently.

## XCF

Gimp has its own file format called XCF. Once you start a new drawing or import an existing photo you will be working with this internal file format.

This file format can store layers, transparency and other attributes of an image. Best practice is always to keep a copy in this format. This way you can go back to your image to do fundamental amendments without the need to redo the image. More will follow on this later.

Once your design project is ready you can export it to popular image formats such as JPEG or PNG.

## Gimp versions

At the time of writing this book the latest available version of Gimp is 2.8.14. Should you run into something that does not work as described in the book please check which version of Gimp you are using.

## How to check your version?

- **Main menu**: *Help > About GIMP*

# Chapter 2: Meet Gimp!

## What you will learn

This chapter introduces the Gimp workspace and demonstrates how to customize the layout.

# Prerequisites

To work with the examples in this book you should already have Gimp installed.

# Workspace layout

This is how Gimp appears on the screen after a successful installation.

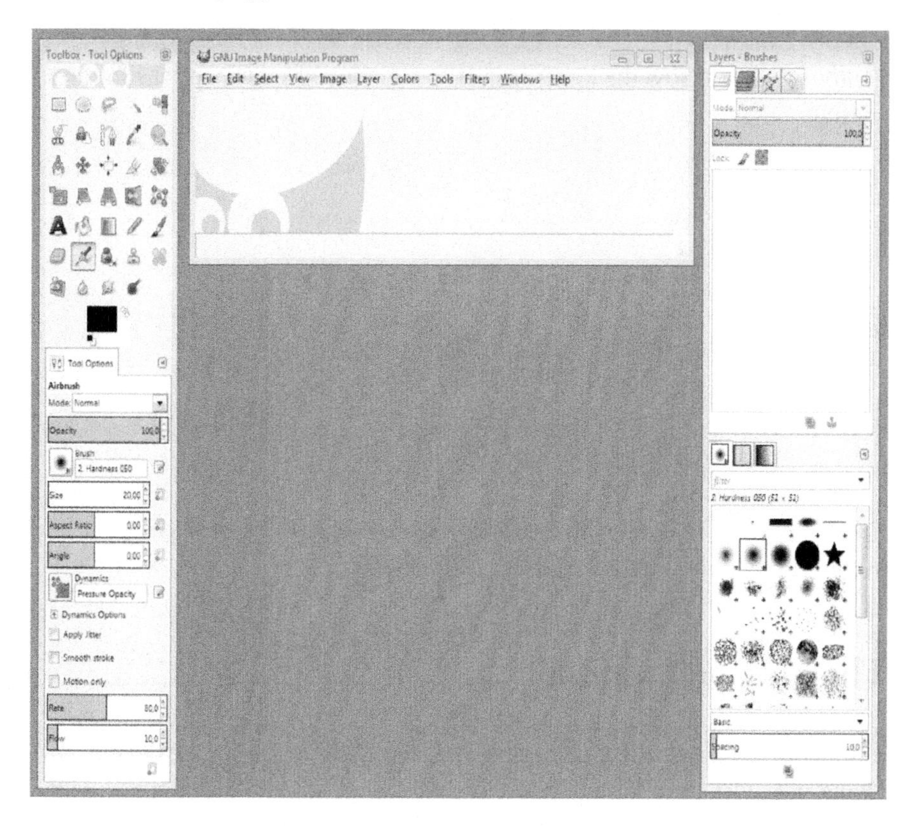


The workspace can be divided into three main windows.

# The "Toolbox - Tool Options" window

This window contains the tools that you will use to draw and to change images.

Note the exact title of the window. The title hints that the window is divided into two parts.

On the top of the window there is a dockable dialogue called *Toolbox* and on the bottom we have the *Tool Options*. These two are related because the *Tool Options* dialogue is content aware. It will display options for whatever tool you selected from the *Toolbox*.

Practice makes perfect, the saying goes, so select the *Text Tool* from the *Toolbox* and note how the lower half of the window displays options for text editing:

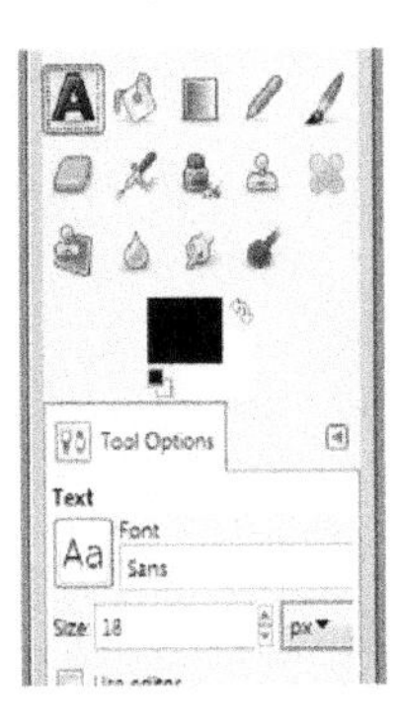


The same thing happens with the other tools as well. Many of those will be introduced later in different chapters of the book.

## The "Image" window

The *Image Window* will appear on the middle of the screen in the default layout of Gimp.

This is where you open existing images or start working on new drawings. If you have just started Gimp you have no images that you are working on hence the window will be empty.

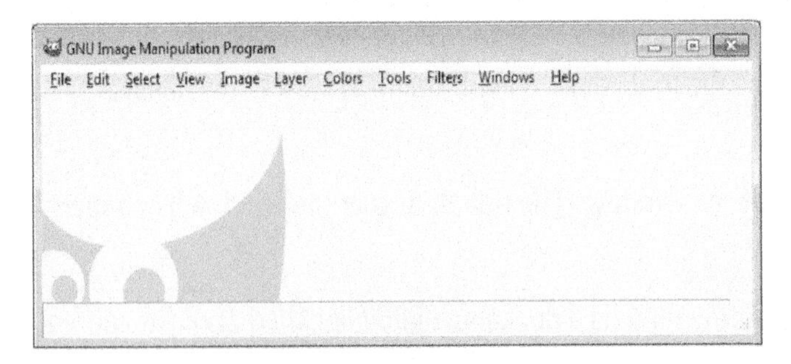

# The "Layers - Brushes" dock

This window is also made up of different parts.

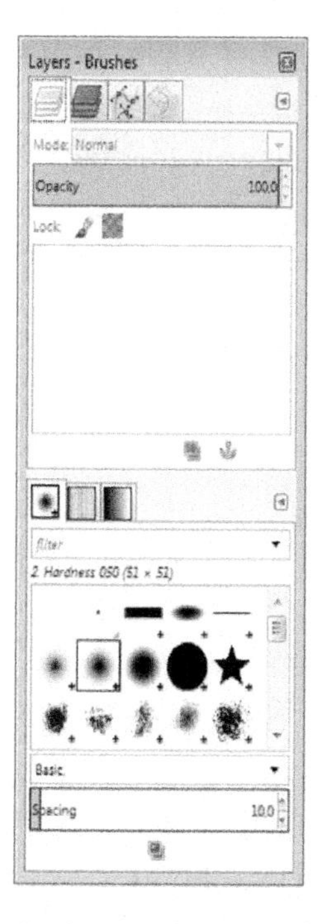


At the top there are four dialogues (Layers, Channels, Paths, Undo) each one dedicated to a different use. We will explore those later in the book.

Feel free to change the active dialogue by clicking on the icons which represent the functions.

The bottom dock groups three more docks (Brushes, Patterns, Gradients).

## Dockable dialogues

Gimp is flexible and can be personalized to great details. All these dockable dialogues can be reorganized. You can move them between docks as you prefer.

If you are new to Gimp you might want to leave things as they are for now. As you get more used to how things work you'll have the possibility to reorganize the layout to your taste.

Also it is worth noting that there are more dialogues you can add to your workspace.

## This is how to do it

- **Main menu**: *Windows > Dockable dialogues*

## Recently closed docks

When I started using Gimp I often closed one of the docks (windows) accidentally.

I wanted to close Gimp and it seemed logical to close all the windows individually. This is not necessary. When you want to close Gimp only close the *Image Window* or do it from the menu.

## This is how to quit

- **Main menu**: *File > Quit*

Anyhow if you've already closed one of the docs don't panic it's easy to get them back.

## This is how to do it

- **Main menu**: *Windows > Recently Closed Docks*

You should see the name of the dock you need to reopen.

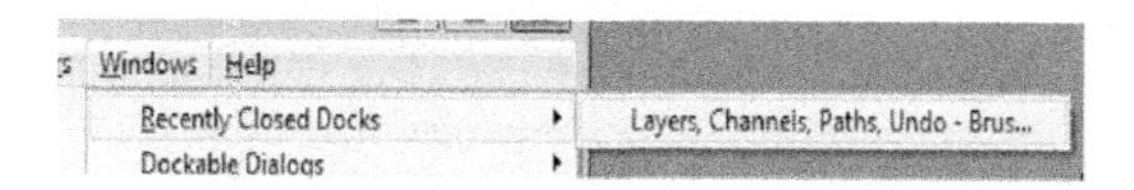

## Single-window mode

In case you cannot get used to the multi window layout of Gimp there is an alternative for you. From version 2.8 it is possible to make all docks grouped into a single window.

## This is how to do it

- **Main menu**: *Windows > Single-Window Mode*

## Hiding docks

Typically you will be switching between tools while working with Gimp. Draw something, crop something else and so on. However if you need a distraction free workspace you can hide the side docks temporarily. Of course you can get them back any time.

## This is how to do it

- **Main menu**: *Windows > Hide Docks*
- **Short cut**: *Tab*

# Chapter 3: Your first drawing

## What you will learn

This chapter demonstrates how to select and operate tools in Gimp.

The goal is to create a simple drawing and save it as an image file. Because Gimp uses its own file format (XCF) it is required to export the image to a common file format such as PNG or JPEG.

# Tools

## Airbrush Tool

As the name suggests you can draw on the canvas the same way as you paint with an airbrush. Operating this tool is quite simple. All you need to do is press and hold down the left mouse button and drag the cursor.

## This is how to access it

In the *Steps* section you will need to select this tool from the *Toolbox*. Below you can find two methods to do that.

- **Toolbox panel**:
- **Short cut**: *A*

These *This is how to ...* elements will reoccur in the book. Where applicable you will find ways to access features from main menu bar or via shortcuts. When using the shortcuts make sure the Gimp application window is in focus.

## Steps

## 0. Start Gimp

Throughout this book it is assumed you have Gimp running.

## 1. Create a new image

## This is how to do it

- **Main menu**: *File > New...*
- **Short cut**: *CTRL + N*

## 2. Specify the image size

When creating a new image you must specify the dimensions (width and height). By default Gimp will ask for these values in terms of pixels. If you prefer to work with inches or millimeters select it in the dropdown next to *Height*.

Enter 200 pixels for the width and the same for the height.

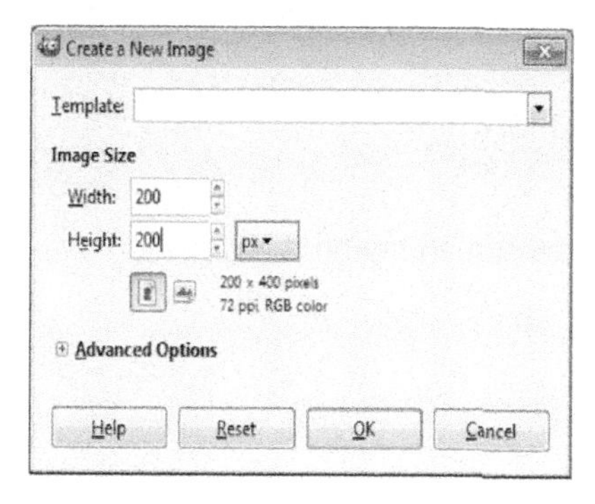

## 3. Understand the coordinate system

Move your mouse over the empty white canvas and see how some numbers are displayed at the bottom left corner. These are the coordinates.

These figure pairs indicate where the mouse cursor is located in your image.

Every pixel in your image has a coordinate. The top left corner is 0,0 where the first number is the horizontal value while the one after the comma is the vertical one.

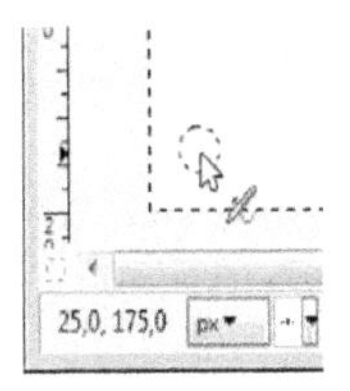


In the example above, my cursor is at the 25th horizontal pixel starting from left and the 175th one starting from the top. Note that the horizontal coordinate is displayed as "25,0". As you move the mouse around you will always see an integer value. If we were to work with inches instead of pixels fractions could also make sense.

## 4. Use the *Airbrush Tool*

Select the *Airbrush Tool* from *Toolbox*. Draw something on the canvas.

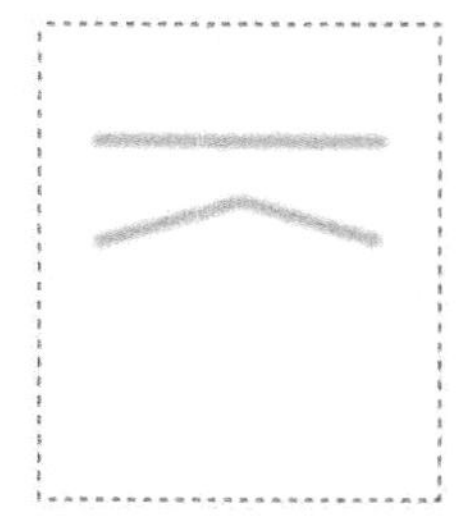

Make as many lines or figures as you like.

What if you wanted to revert your latest move? Of course, you can *undo* changes.

## This is how to do it

- **Main menu**: *Edit > Undo*
- **Short cut**: *CTRL + Z*

You can 'undo' multiple steps which essentially allows you to go back to earlier versions of your image.

The undoable steps however are only kept as long as Gimp is running. If you quit Gimp this history will be lost.

# 5. Save your drawing

Once you are done with your current drawing you need to save it.

## This is how to do it

- **Main menu**: *File > Save*
- **Short cut**: *CTRL + S*

Enter a name of your choice such as 'firstdrawing.xcf'.

When we **save** an image it's always done in Gimp's internal file format which is XCF. This file format is used to store your graphic design projects made with Gimp.

## 6. Export to PNG

If you want to insert your drawing into your presentation or display it on your website you need to export it from Gimp.

## This is how to do it

- **Main menu**: *File > Export as...*
- **Short cut**: *CTRL + Shift + E*

The easiest way to select your target image format is to define the file extension along with the name. Example: holidayphoto.png will hint Gimp to export it into PNG format. Continue by clicking on the *Export* button.

If you want to export to a different format like JPEG specify the filename as holidayphoto.jpg.

In the next window you can fine tweak the conversion details based on what type of format you are exporting to.

For now leave all values as they are and click on *Export*.

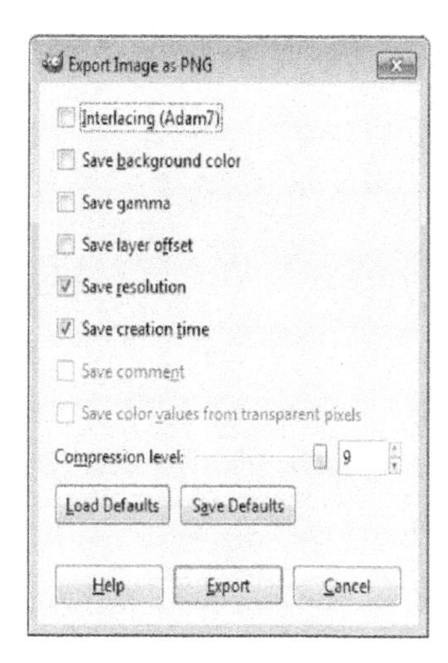

## 7. Close your work!

Now that your drawing is complete and saved it's time to clean up the workspace. Let's close the current image.

## This is how to do it

- **Main menu**: *File > Close View*
- **Short cut**: *CTRL + W*

If you try to close without saving first you will be asked to save first or discard your image.

## 8. Congratulations!

That was quick! You've just learnt how to create a new image, draw something and export to PNG file format!

# Chapter 4: Convert to black and white

## What you will learn

In this chapter you will learn two distinct ways of converting a colour image to black and white. The first method is more simple while the second one gives you more control over the details.

## Image used for the exercise

Source: *Hermann* pixabay.com

## First approach: Converting to grayscale

Images can be stored in different colour modes. Gimp gives you a choice of three.

- **RGB**: in this (default) colour mode the pixels that make up your image are coloured using the three primary colours: **R**ed, **G**reen and **B**lue. Any time you are not sure what to use, use this mode.
- **Indexed**: in this mode the image will be made up of a pre-selected number of colours only. The advantage is that this format can yield an extremely compact image file.
- **Grayscale**: this mode contains a 'colour' palette of 256 levels of gray.

# Steps

## 1. Open your image

### This is how to do it

- **Main menu**: *File > Open*
- **Short cut**: *CTRL + O*

Based on the size of your image Gimp might change the zoom settings for you automatically. The zoom level will be calculated based on the available space. If the image is bigger than the size of your *Image Window* Gimp will zoom out for you and vice versa. In my case Gimp displayed the image with a 66.7% zoom level to fit the window.

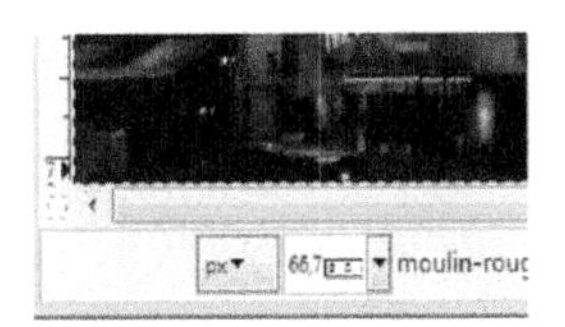

If you resize your window align the zoom settings might make sense. The easiest way to do that is using the autozoom feature.

### This is how to do it

- **Main menu**: *View > Zoom > Fit Image in Window*
- **Short cut**: *CTRL + Shift + J*

## 2. Convert to grayscale

### This is how to do it

- **Main menu**: *Image > Mode > Grayscale*

The image is now in grayscale mode.

## 3. Export

Export your image as a PNG or save it as a Gimp file (.xcf).

## Second approach: Black and white using the channel mixer

**Note**: Coming from the *First approach* please start over with the coloured image. This method only works with images that are **not** in grayscale mode.

This option gives you more control over the end result. You can amend the colour levels or the luminosity.

## Steps

## 1. Open your file

## 2. Open the channel mixer

## This is how to do it

- **Main menu**: *Colors > Components > Channel Mixer...*

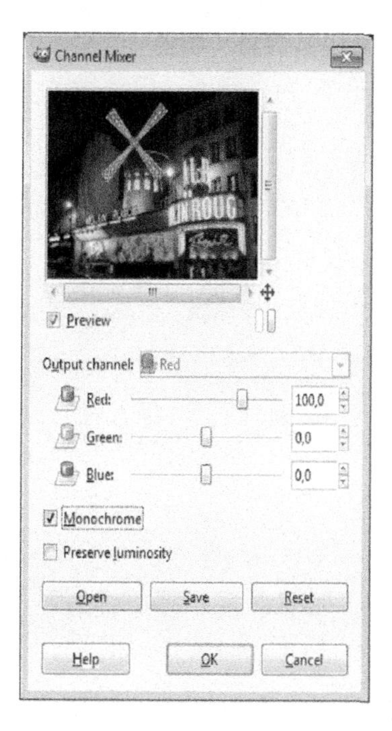


## 3. Select the *Monochrome* option

This converts to monochrome colour.

## 4. Fine-tune the image using the sliders

Start moving the sliders and check what you see in the *Preview Window*. When satisfied press *OK*.

> The *Preview Window* is a recurring element in the dialogue windows where you alter your image. Provided the *Preview* checkbox is selected your changes will update the small preview area. If you don't want to apply the current changes on the image click on *Cancel*.

## 5. Export

Export your image as a PNG or save it as a Gimp file (.xcf).

# Chapter 5: New image from selection

## What you will learn

This chapter teaches you how to use a part of an existing photo and save it as a new one.

This technique can serve you well in many different situations. You can create a cover image for social media sites. Or maybe you need to send a screenshot to your system administrator - but you don't want to send an image of your whole desktop. Instead you want to 'cut out' the relevant parts and save them as new image.

# Image used for the exercise

# Tools

## Rectangle Selection Tool

Often times, all we need to do is edit a section of an image. In these cases we can select the necessary region using one of the selection tools.

For this job the *Rectangle Selection* tool is the most straightforward one. As the name suggests a rectangular shape can be selected. It's great when we want to apply certain changes to the selection (eg. paint with colour) or to create a new image from the selection.

## This is how to access it

- **Toolbox panel**:
- **Short cut**: *R*

To create a selection press and hold the left mouse button and draw a rectangle.

This is how a selection looks like:

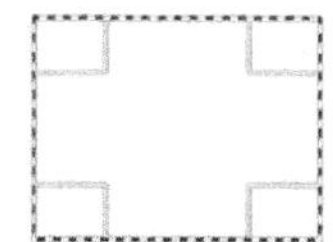

You will be able to change the selection you've created as long as you don't create a new one. To resize the selection you can click into one of the four corners and drag the mouse to make the selection smaller or larger. If you want to move the selection by hand, move the mouse to the center of the rectangle and start dragging the selection.

## Tool Options Panel

This panel is content aware. Based on the type of tool you are using, different options will be shown. Within the *Rectangle Selection* tool, you can alter the dimensions and the position of the selection in this panel.

## Facebook cover image attributes

As it can be easily found out from Facebook's help, a cover photo needs to be 851 pixels wide and 315 pixels high.

> It goes without saying that it is not a must to crop your image in advance when creating a cover photo for Facebook. If you upload a highres photo (which is likely the case if you work with a digital camera) you can select the part that should be used. But the method you will learn here can be useful for other sites or problems as well.

## Steps

### 1. Open your file

### 2. Select the *Rectangle Selection* tool from the *Toolbox*

### 3. Draw a rectangle selection

Start creating a rectangle by pressing and holding the left mouse button and dragging your cursor.

Notice that the *Tool options* gets updated as you change the selection. The fields indicating the size will guide you to create a properly sized selection. Does if feel a little cumbersome to get the dimensions right this way?

### 4. Define the exact dimensions

Enter 851 pixels for the width and 315 pixels for the height of the selection in the *Toolbox Panel*. The selection window is automatically resized over the image.

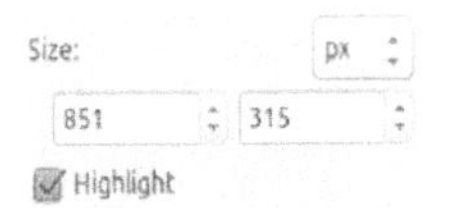


> Notice that I also selected the *Highlight* option from the *Tool options Panel*. This feature offers a better visibility of what is currently selected. Don't be afraid, it won't alter the image in any way. You can turn it off if you find it annoying.

## 5. Move the selection

Move the selection over the region you want to use for your cover photo. Do that by dragging the selection or by entering position coordinates into the *Tool Options Panel*.

## 6. Copy the selection to the clipboard

Make sure you have the selection in focus (click in to the selection by the mouse). Now copy the selection to the clipboard.

## This is how to do it

- **Main menu**: *Edit > Copy*
- **Short cut**: *CTRL + C*

## 7. Paste as new

## This is how to do it

- **Main menu**: *Edit > Paste as > New Image*

- **Short cut**: *CTRL + Shift + V*

Gimp now opens a new *Image Window*. That said you now learnt that it's possible to edit multiple images simultaneously. The new window shows the content of the clipboard - which is your selection.

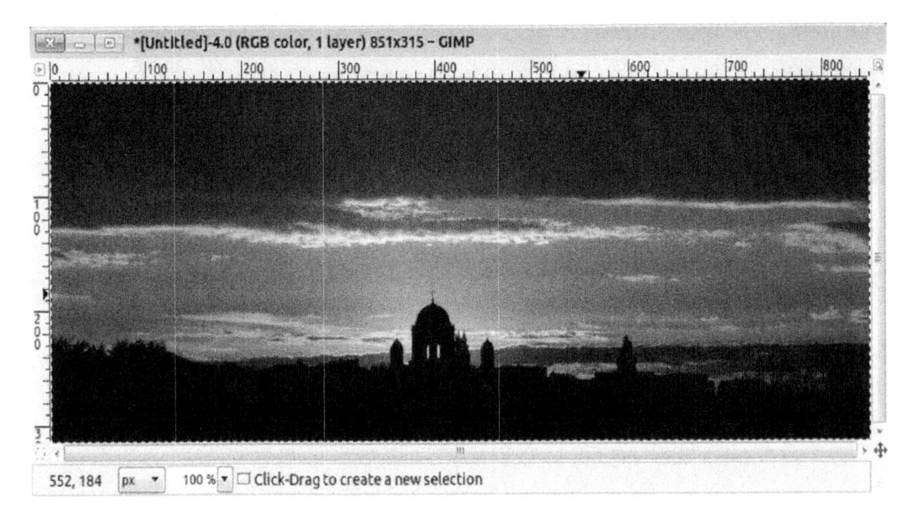


## 8. Export

Export your image as a PNG or save it as a Gimp file (.xcf).

> How is it going so far? I wrote this book to help you get started with photo editing and graphic design. Should you run into any problems, please come and visit me at Facebook or G+.

# Chapter 6: Resizing images

## What you will learn

This chapter illustrates how Gimp can be used to resize images. I will briefly introduce you to the concepts that one needs to know for doing proper resizing.

# Image used for the exercise

The width of the image used in this example is 1280 px and it has a height of 853 pixels. This is a good resolution for prints for example. The higher the resolution the larger the size of the image file.

This can be an issue if you store a great number of them and would only use them in a scaled version anyway.

## Aspect ratio

Every image has a value that represents the proportion between its height and width. Have a look at this ball, for example:

This ball has an *aspect ratio* of 1:1 which means that its height equals to its width.

This is not the case for every image of course.

The truck shown above has a width about twice its height. Hence its aspect ratio is close to 2:1.

When resizing images you need to make sure the aspect ratio is respected and kept through the process.

If we change only the width of the image and leave the height as it is the ratio will change and we will have a deformed ball.

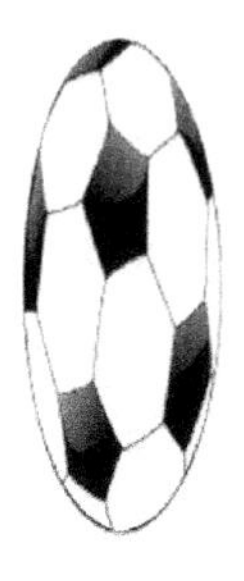

The same holds true when changing the height only.

Gimp can help us maintain this ratio. When defining the value for one dimension the counterpart will be calculated for us automatically.

> Note the math behind the aspect ratio. If we were to change the two dimensions (width, height) by hand we need to enter values properly calculated. If you start with an image that is 1050x700 pixels the aspect ratio is 15:10. Let's say we remove 100 from each dimensions: we get 950x600. The aspect ratio is about 15.8:10 resulting in a deformed image!

# Steps

# 1. Open your file

# 2. Scale the image

# This is how to access it

- **Main menu**: *Image > Scale Image*

This window will help us set the new dimensions. In the *Width* and *Height* boxes you can see a button showing a chain. This button tells Gimp to keep the aspect ratio during the resizing process.

The chain button has two states. You need to keep the chain closed in order to have Gimp help you out with the values.

Note that if you enter a value in the *Width* box and click into the *Height* box the value is auto calculated. This also works the other way around. After you are familiar with how it works enter a width. In the example I entered 127.

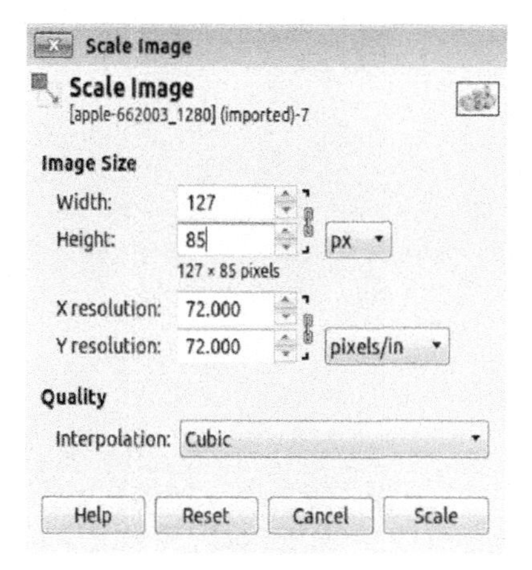


After moving the cursor to the *Height* box it is auto calculated and shows 85 pixels.

## 3. Click the *Scale* button

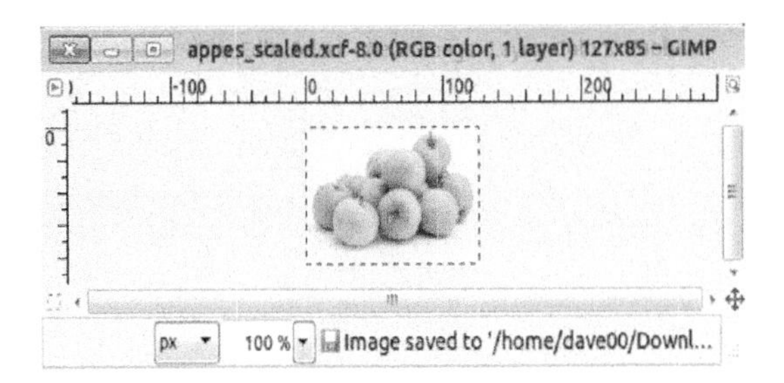


The image is now scaled and the new dimensions are 127 by 85 pixels. This a small image with a compact size!

## 4. Export

Export your image as a PNG or save it as a Gimp file (.xcf).

# Chapter 7: Transparent background

## What you will learn

This chapter goes over some advanced methods (compared to the previous exercises).

# Image used for the exercise

Source: *PublicDomainPictures* pixabay.com

## Images with background colour

Not every image has a background colour but those which do come with limitations with regards to usability. Have a look at this little guy:

Source: downloads (original source unknown but please let me know so I can give credit)

The image of the little fellow is good as long as we use it on a white background. But if we try to put it on some kind of coloured material the issue becomes clear.

That is an ugly image of a giant penguin taking over a city!

What we need is a version of the image that contains the pixels of the penguin but not the white background.

Note that not every image format will let you use transparency. One of the reasons we are using PNG in this book is because it does.

# Tools

## Fuzzy Select Tool

We already learned how to use the *Rectangle Select Tool* which is great to select regions by dimension. Let's add something else to our arsenal. The *Fuzzy Selection Tool* can select regions of your image by matching colours or similarity.

## This is how to access it

- **Toolbox panel**:
- **Short cut**: *U*

## Steps

## 1. Open your file

First we will work with the image of penguin. From the downloads please open *chapter-7-penguin.png*.

## 2. Add alpha channel to create a transparent layer

## This is how to access it

- **Main menu**: *Layer > Transparency > Add Alpha Channel*

The alpha channel is the layer that will provide you the transparency. An image with a single layer without the alpha channel cannot be transparent.

## 3. Remove the white background

Select the *Fuzzy Select Tool* and click anywhere on the white background. It will be indicated as highlighted.

Press *Delete* to remove the selection.

## 4. Detect the edges

Now all that's left are the pixels that make up the little penguin. Let's have a closer look at the edges of the figure.

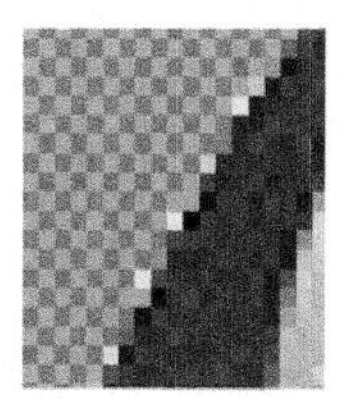

As you can see the edges are sharp and still contain some tone of white and gray. If we were to use the image on the city background it would still stand out a bit.

## 5. Select the transparent background

Just as you did with the white background now select the empty space around the penguin using the *Fuzzy Select Tool*.

## 6. Invert the selection

## This is how to do it

- **Main menu**: *Select > Invert*
- **Short cut**: *Ctrl + I*

Now the shape of the penguin is selected.

## 7. Create a border for the selection

We need to create a border selection along the lines of the figure.

# This is how to do it

- **Main menu**: *Select > Border*

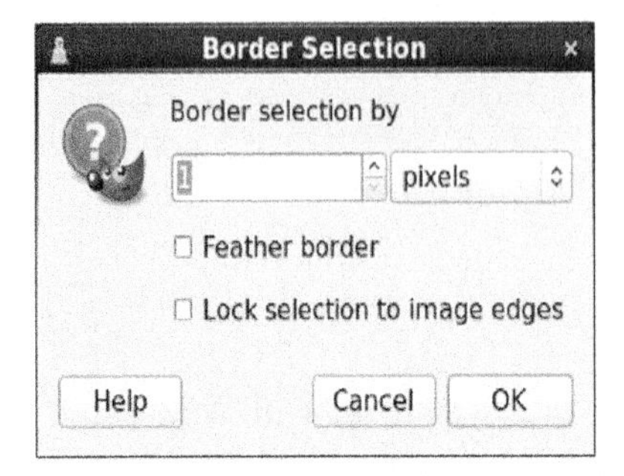


Set 1 pixel for the border size then click *OK*.

# 8. Blur!

Filters in Gimp are similar to the tools we've already used but typically they would alter the material with an effect. One such effect is the blur effect which can be used to smoothen a region.

You should still have the border selection active when you apply the filter.

# This is how to do it

- **Main menu**: *Filters > Blur > Blur*

Now the colour differences should be smoothened along the edges of the figure. Depending on the image you are working with you might need to use a different border size. At this point you have an image that has a transparent background. Feel free to save or export the "transparent penguin image" as usual.

It would be more interesting though to combine this one with the image of the city.

# 10. Open the image of the city

We already know that Gimp can handle multiple *Image Windows* at once. Just to revise, to do that, leave the penguin and open the image of the city as well.

# This is how to do it

- **Main menu**: *File > Open*
- **Short cut**: *CTRL + O*

You should see two *Image Windows* now.

# 11. Clear the active selections

We need to make sure there are no active selections. This could be a problem since in a bit we will need to select the whole content of the penguin image.

Select the *Image Window* where you have the image of the penguin. Now deactivate all selections.

## This is how to do it

- **Main menu**: *Select > None*
- **Short cut**: *CTRL + Shift + A*

Why do we need to do this? If you have an active selection and try to put something on the clipboard, Gimp will record the content of the selection and not the whole image.

## 12. Copy the content to the clipboard

Now copy the image to the clipboard.

## This is how to do it

- **Main menu**: *Edit > Copy*
- **Short cut**: *CTRL + C*

## 13. Paste

Select the other *Image Window* where you have the image of the city. Simply paste the content of the clipboard.

## This is how to do it

- **Main menu**: *Edit > Paste*
- **Short cut**: *CTRL + V*

# 14. Flatten the image

The penguin now overflows the city, but the two are not merged properly. Yet.

Checkout the *Layers Dialog*.

> If you don't see the *Layers Dialog* you can try to bring it back with *CTRL + L*.

## This is how to anchor the floating layer

- **Main menu**: *Layer > Anchor Layer*
- **Layer dialog**: Right click on the floating layer > *Anchor Layer*

Don't panic but I think there is a giant penguin walking around the city!

# Chapter 8: Combining monochrome with colours

## What you will learn

This chapter describes the basics of working with layers. On top of that, you will learn how to deliver one of the most commonly used photo retouching effect. That is turning a coloured photograph into it's monochrome version, but let some parts remain coloured. For this we will apply a layer mask on the image.

> Although you might be reading this book on a monochrome device the steps are intentionally put together so that you can follow them.

## Image used for the exercise

Source: *knerri61* pixabay.com

# Layers

Gimp's native format, the XCF supports a technique called layering. Dividing your image into layers allows you to edit the building blocks separately.

Just to see a simple example have look at this image:

Without layers, we could hardly replace the background, without completely redoing the image.

If we break the image up into layers we have the background layer:

And the penguin:

These two layers can be saved together in the XCF format. If you want to use the image in its current form for your presentation, or on a website, you simply have to export as we've learnt already.

> Although the layer with the penguin is shown in front of a white background, that is only an indication. The surroundings of the penguin must be transparent. You've already learnt the technique to create transparency in the previous chapter.

When you are working with layers in Gimp all the available layers are listed in the *Layers Dialog*.

In our example, the order of the layers from bottom to top is how they are placed on each other. The background layer has no transparency. If we'd change the order of the two we would only see the grass, but not the penguin.

Let's look into the tools necessary for this project.

# Tools

## Paintbrush tool

One of the tools in Gimp's arsenal for drawing is the *Paintbrush tool*. We can use it to paint specific regions of an image with a colour. It will have a key role in creating the "see through" effect later on, when we get to working with the layer mask.

## This is how to access it

- **Toolbox panel**:
- **Short cut**: *P*

## Steps

# 0. Ensure alpha channel

In order to create an image with transparent background, it has to have an alpha channel.

While the image referenced for the exercise has one, this is something you need to keep in mind for your future projects.

**This is how to check if your layer has an alpha channel**

- **Main menu**: *Layer > Transparency > Add Alpha Channel*
- **Layer dialog**: Right click on the layer > *Add Alpha Channel*

In case the option is not available (grayed out), it simply means the alpha channel is already there.

# 1. Open the photo file

# 2. Duplicate the image layer

Checkout the layer window. Currently there is one layer that has the name of the image. This is the default but, can be changed.

The part where most people break up with Gimp, is when they try to work with one of the tools, but they are working on the wrong layer. That is why you always want to make sure, you have the proper layer activated.

Activate your layer on the layer dialog, simply by clicking on it once, just as you would do with a file.

Now we can duplicate it.

## This is how to do it

- **Main menu**: *Layer > Duplicate Layer*
- **Layer dialog**: Right click on the layer > *Duplicate Layer*

Now you should have two identical layers. The only difference between them is their name.

Notice the little eye icon on the left. To help you focus Gimp allows you to temporarily hide any of the layers. Only those with the icon shown are displayed in the *Image Window*. Feel free to check how it works by switching the visibility on and off for the two layers. Turn both back to visible before you continue though.

## 3. Make the top layer monochrome

This is the point where you want to be careful. Make sure the the top layer by selecting it in the layer window.

Use the *Channel Mixer* (feel free to look back to Chapter 4) to make this layer monochrome.

# 4. Add a layer mask to the top layer

Now we have a top layer that is black and white, and we have a lower layer that is coloured.

The goal would be to make the top level transparent where the stop sign is red, so the colour can come through from the lower layer. A *Layer Mask* is just what we need.

# This is how to do add a layer mask

- **Main menu**: *Layer > Mask > Add Layer Mask...*
- **Layer dialog**: Right click on the layer > *Add Layer Mask...*

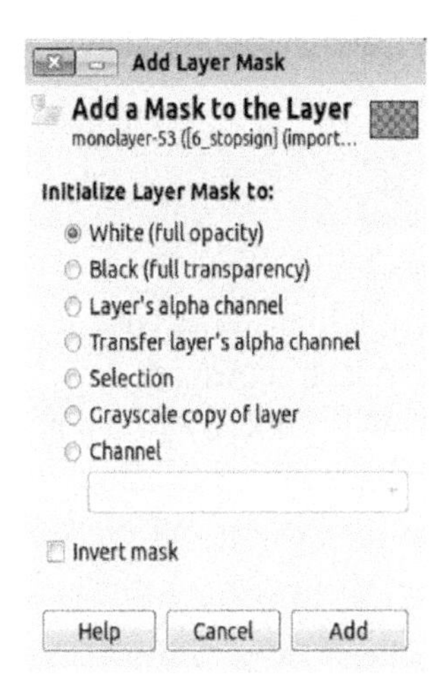


We need our layer mask to be completely opaque by default (this is the opposite of transparent). Colours have different meaning in this context. In our example "white" means opaque.

Later when we paint over the layer mask with black, that is where the mask will let colours come through from the lower layer.

Leave the options as they are and click *Add* to create the mask.

The mask should be shown as white box next to your monochrome layer in the layer dialog.

## 5. Select the *Paintbrush Tool* tool from the *Toolbox*

## 6. Choose black as your foreground colour

Have a look at the colour picker tool in the Toolbox.

This utility can be familiar to you if you worked with MS Paint before.

The rectangle on the left (blue in the example) shows the current foreground colour.

The one on the right displays our current background colour.

Click on any of them to bring up the colour picker wizard.

Here is a tip for you. In the bottom left corner there are two smaller squares, black and white respectively. If at any time you wish to reset your colours, click on the little squares.

For our current exercise we also need black as the foreground colour, so if you don't already have that, give this feature a test drive.

## 7. Activate the layer mask

We are about to paint on the layer mask. Click on the layer mask to activate it. Otherwise you will paint over one of the "real" layers.

## 8. Paint the stop sign

This is the part where you actually need to paint with the *Paintbrush Tool*. It is surprisingly easy.

Press and hold your left mouse button and move the mouse to paint a line. Don't worry about getting it right the first time. Feel free to make some experiments. You can always revert your steps.

## This is how to undo

- **Main menu**: *Edit > Undo Paintbrush*
- **Short cut**: *CTRL + Z*

Try painting the stop sign carefully, so it's red colour becomes visible.

Notice that wherever you go with your mouse, it leaves a black line on the layer mask.

The contrast between the black and the white creates the *see through* effect. Finish by painting the shape of the sign.

As you might have already guessed, the world is not only black and white. Actually I meant to say, the layer mask can be painted with other colours.

If you apply shades of gray on the layer mask, you can create semi-transparent parts.

## 9. Export

Export your image as a PNG or save it as a Gimp file (.xcf).

# Chapter 9: Design an ebook cover

## What you will learn

In this chapter you'll study how to combine what we learnt so far for an advanced design project. After you finish this exercise you will know how to start with multi layered designs.

> Although you might be reading this book on a monochrome device the steps are intentionally put together in a way that you can still follow them.

## Image used for the exercise

Source: *avantrend* pixabay.com

## Attributes of the cover

*"Never judge a book by its cover"* the saying goes.

While this holds true in many cases, most people actually judge by the first impression. Especially in the case of real books. Where the first impression is the cover. At least I do jump on attractive covers for sure.

A compelling cover should definitely have an image. For the dimensions we should go with a portrait layout. We will create a cover that is 600 pixels wide and 800 pixels high. Most probably you are going to aim for a resolution bigger than that. But since the principles are the same please apply the figures for your case.

# Tools

## Blend Tool

This utility (also called *The Gradient Tool*) allows you to draw a gradient transitioning effect between colours.

## This is how to access it

- **Toolbox panel**:
- **Short cut**: *L*

## Bucket Fill Tool

This tool should be used whenever you need to paint a region to a solid colour.

## This is how to access it

- **Toolbox panel**:
- **Short cut**: *Shift + B*

## Align Tool

Similar to how you can align text in a word processor you can align objects in Gimp. In case of our ebook cover we will align the text properly to the center.

## This is how to access it

- **Toolbox panel**:

- **Short cut**: *Q*

## Colour Picker Tool

In Gimp you can work with the predefined colours or mix a new one for your needs.

But what if you need to work with a colour that is present in your image already? The *Colour Picker Tool* allows you to 'pick' colours from opened images to be able to use as your foreground or background colours.

Otherwise you might have a hard time trying to mix the proper colour definition.

## This is how to access it

- **Toolbox panel**:
- **Short cut**: *O*

## Text Tool

Whenever you want to add some text to your image you should go with the *Text Tool*. It is important to keep in mind that every text element you add will be added as a new layer.

## This is how to access it

- **Toolbox panel**:
- **Short cut**: *T*

## Move Tool

As it says on the tin we can use the *Move Tool* to change the position of selected elements.

## This is how to access it

- **Toolbox panel**:
- **Short cut**: *M*

## Steps

## 1. Open the photo file

## 2. Resize the canvas

The image that I used in the example has a resolution of 640x344 pixels. We need to change that so that the actual drawing area is 600x800 pixels.

This special area is called the canvas and we can change the dimensions of it to enlarge or reduce the drawing area. Of course reducing might mean we loose some of the drawing.

Our target width is 600 pixels but the image we use is 640 pixels wide. After examining the image it makes sense to cut 40 pixels from the right side rather than resizing it.

## This is how to do it

- **Main menu**: *Image > Canvas Size...*

Now enter the 600 pixels for the width then 800 pixels for the height. As we anticipated the new canvas size is a lot taller than the original height of our cover photo.

We can now specify where we want to position the photo on the new canvas. One way to do this is to drag the image by the mouse. If you'd rather do it more precisely use the "Offset" values. I put 0 for "Offset X" which means the left border of the cover photo matches the left edge of the canvas and 250 for the "Offset Y" so the photo is placed a little bit towards the bottom of the canvas.

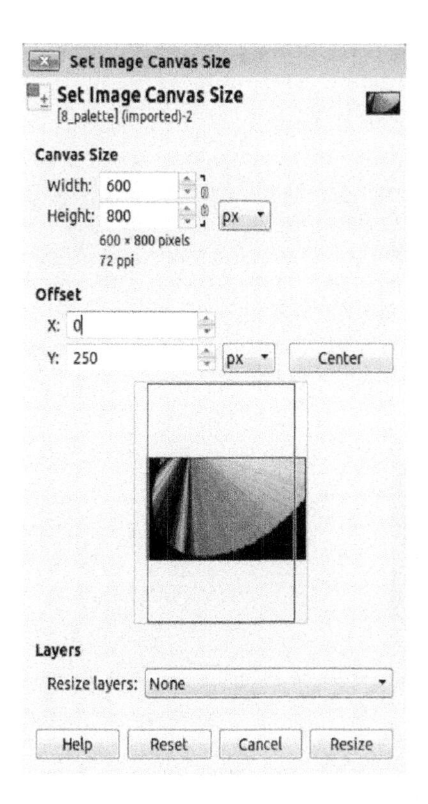


The way you identify a place has nothing to do with science: I used these values because I've already figured out how to use the rest of the canvas.

Here is the cover after resizing:

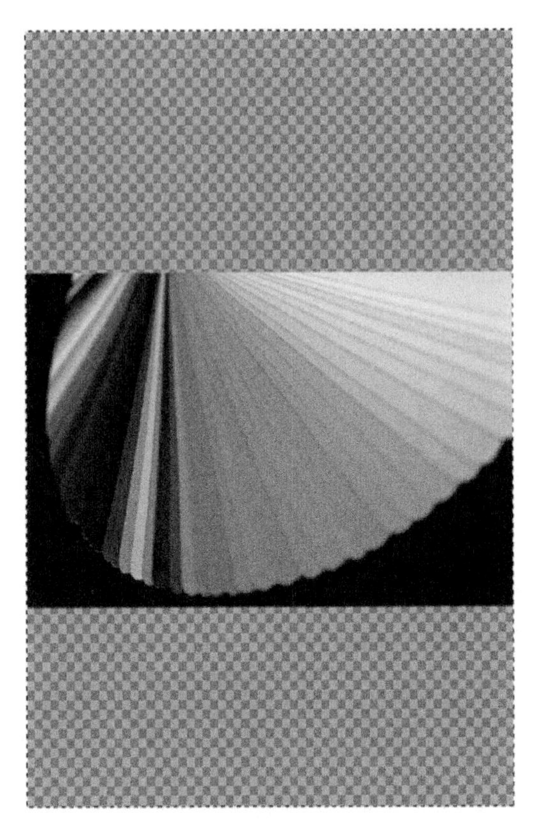

> Make sure you understand the difference between scaling your image and resizing your canvas. Scaling the image means we resize the image matrix so it fits into the new resolution. On the contrary, the way we resize the "Canvas" in this example is like extending the drawing area.

In our book cover example we started off with an image that has a landscape layout but the desired cover image shall be in portrait. To achieve this, we enlarge the canvas size vertically and crop it horizontally a bit.

Now the canvas might not fit into your *Image Window*. Of course you can use the sliders on the sides to move around your image, but if you want to see all your artwork fit the *Image Window* use the proper zoom features.

## This is how to do it

- **Main menu**: *View > Zoom > Fit Image in Window*
- **Shortcut**: *CTRL + Shift + J*

# 3. Create the background layer

In this step we need to create a new layer that should serve as the background colour for the cover.

# This is how to do it

- **Layer Window**:

Now you should see the *Layer creation wizard*:

Set the layer name to "background".

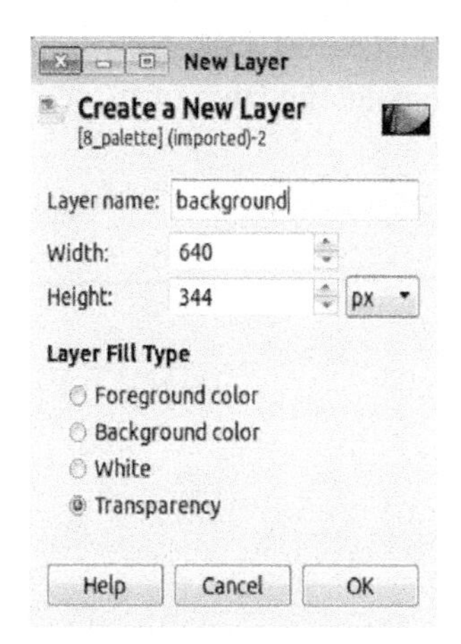


As we can see this layer is now on top of the original layer where the cover photo resides.

Move this layer down.

## This is how to do it

- **Layer Window**: 
- **Mouse**: drag it down with the mouse

The "background" layer should now be the first from the bottom:

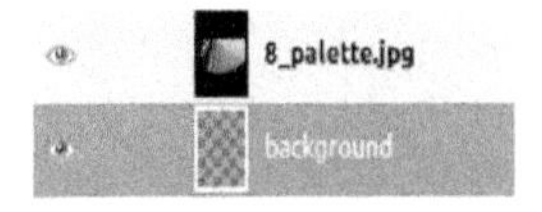


# 4. Paint the background layer

In this step we need to paint the "background" layer black.

Make sure you have the "background" layer selected in the *Layers Panel*.

Select black as your foreground colour and use the *Bucket Fill Tool*. Now by left clicking on the image use the *Bucket Fill Tool* to paint the layer black.

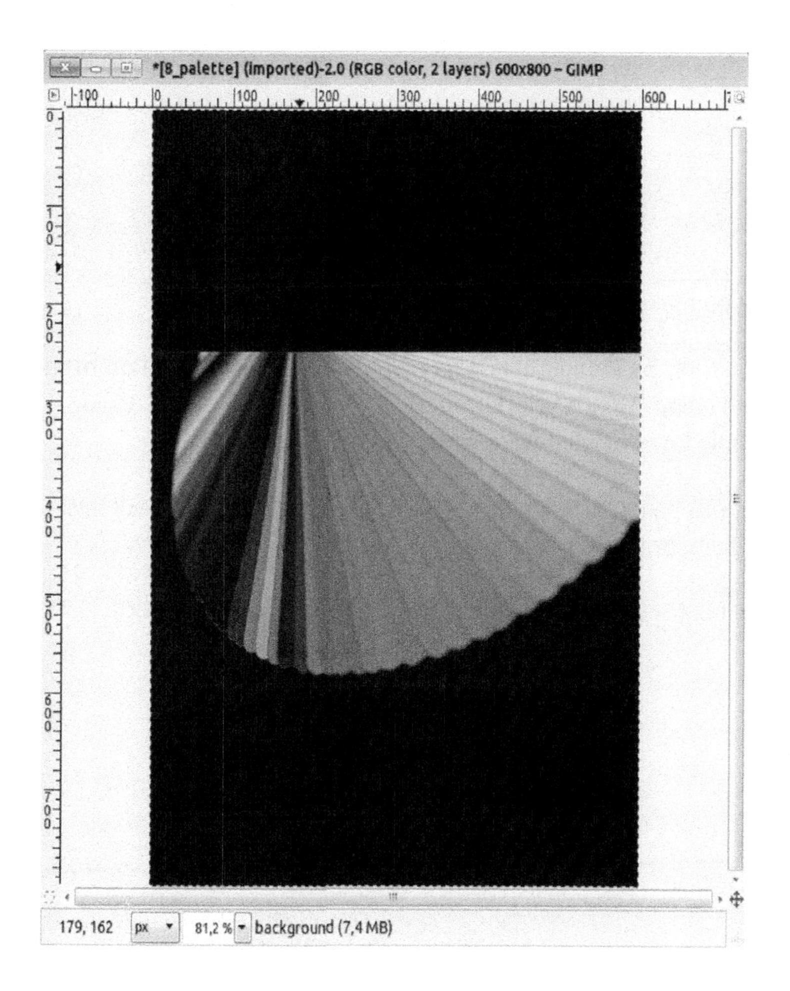


# 5. Smoothing the edges

While the background layer and the cover photo are similar as they both have a black background colour, they do not integrate smoothly.

On the top of the photo there is a firm 'edge'. We don't need to remove it as it can be used as a separator for the top content.

Whereas the lower part of the photo does not integrate well. We will use the *Blend tool* to make a nice gradient colour transition that tricks the eye.

Create a new layer called "gradient". It's okay if this is the top most layer. We will add effects to this layer that should be displayed on top of the others.

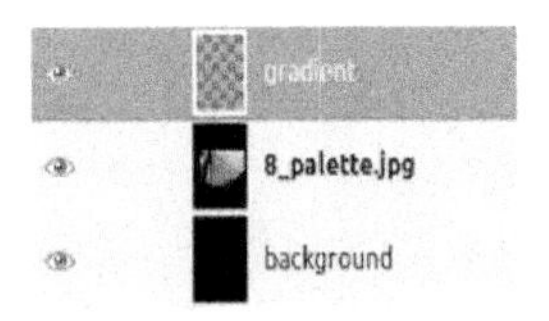


Before moving on make sure you have the "gradient" layer selected.

Select the *Blend tool*. By default the *Blend tool* would create a transition from the "Foreground colour" to the "Background colour". In our case this would result in the whole layer painted with a gradient effect.

In the *Tool Options* panel there are advanced options available to tweak this tool. Click on the button next to the label that says "FG to BG".

In the dropdown list select "FG to Transparent" (FG means foreground).

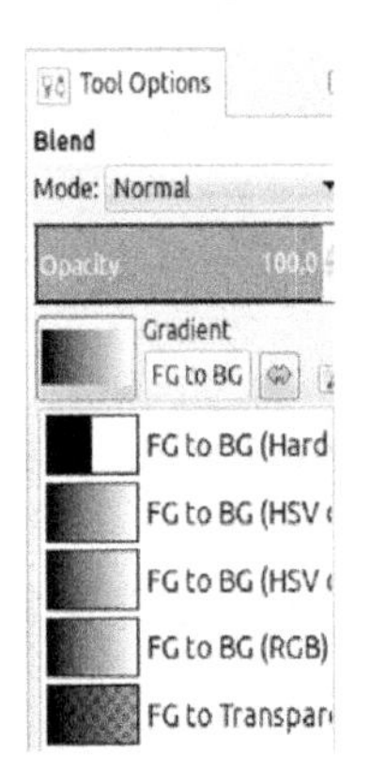


Make sure you have black as your foreground colour.

This way when your create the gradient effect it will start with the "Foreground colour" (black in our case) and gently fade out.

Now using your mouse 'draw' blend lines. Start from the bottom left corner of the image and by holding your left mouse button draw a line diagonally towards the colour palette on the photo. When you release the mouse button the blending effect will be applied.

Doesn't work? Make sure you are applying the *Blend Tool* on the layer we labeled 'gradient' that is the top most one.

Try to draw short lines for a smooth transition. Try to avoid applying the gradient effect over the beautiful coloured palette.

If you want to revert a step at any point while working with the *Blend Tool* (technically any tool) feel free to revert your steps.

## This is how to do it

- **Main menu**: *Edit > Undo*
- **Short cut**: *CTRL + Z*

## 6. Create the title border

Our book cover will have the tone of two main colours (other than the palette). Black is already there. The other colour will be orange. In this step we need to create a coloured rectangle on the top of the cover.

As you might have guessed we need to start by creating a new layer. Let's call it "learn".

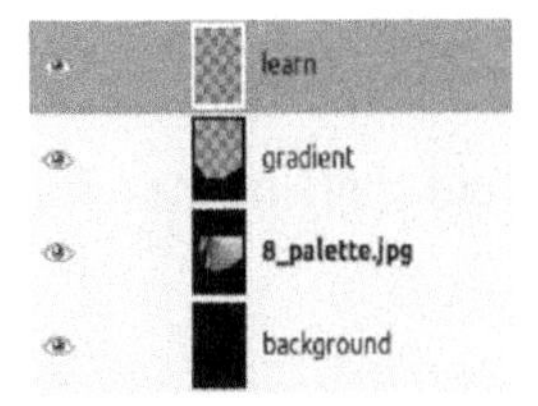


Select the *Rectangle Selection Tool.*

Draw a rectangle that is wider than the canvas and the height is proportionally about 1/10 of the "Canvas" height. Don't be afraid to make the selection larger than the dimensions of the image:

# 7. Paint the title border

The palette image has many strong colours. Let's use one of those to paint this title border.

Select the layer where you have the cover photo (labeled as *palette* on the screenshots). Use the *Colour Picker Tool* to choose a colour. If you are on the right layer, and the picker tool is activated, simply click on any of the coloured areas on the photo to grab a sample. The colour selection panel will indicate that your foreground colour changed.

Activate the "learn" layer again.

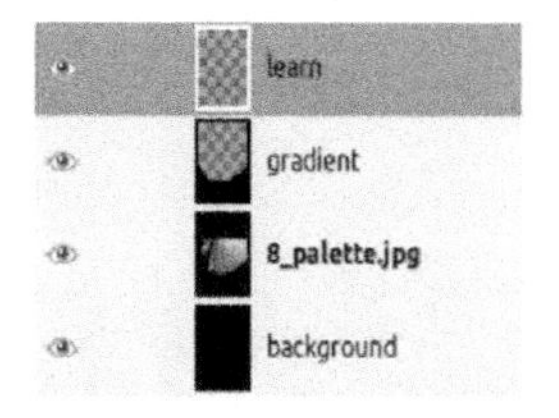


Use the *Bucket Fill Tool* to paint your selection with the new foreground colour.

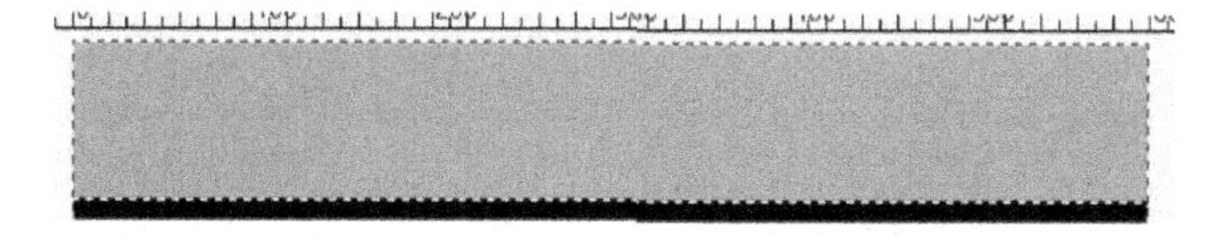

# 8. Add the title text "LEARN"

Set black as your foreground colour.

Select the *Text Tool* and draw a text box over the painted area. The width can be about 1/3 of the available space and the height a little less than what's available.

Type "LEARN" into your text box.

Try to vary the font size so it looks similar to mine. To change the font size:

- click into your text box
- select all your text with the mouse
- in the *Tool Options* panel change the font size

Now try to resize the text box gently so it is just big enough to show every letter inside.

> Font face matters: in the example I used a true-type font called "Prototype". If you want to use a different type just change it similarly to how you altered the font size.

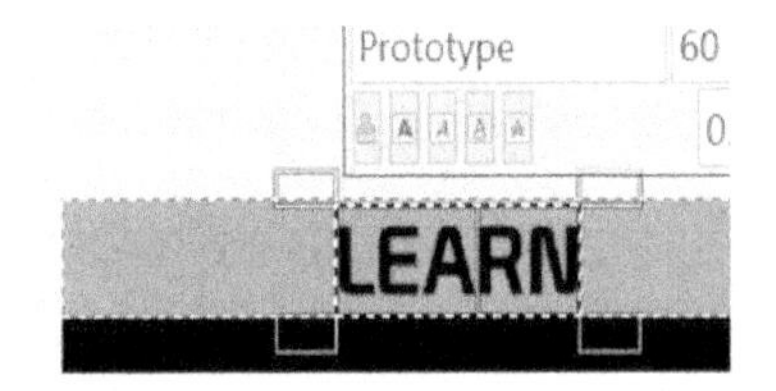


## 9. Align the text vertically

Inside the orange bar we need to align the text vertically. But there's no need to be 100% precise at this step.

Select the *Move Tool*. Press and hold the left mouse button to move your text box. Try to position it vertically roughly in the middle inside the orange bar.

> Having problems moving the text only? Don't worry this is very common. When moving text around make sure you actually click on one of the letters and not the layer behind the letters. Extra tip for you: try to hold the *Shift* button while moving things around. This way Gimp will only move the currently selected layer.

## 10. Align the text horizontally

Aligning the text vertically was easy and we could get away simply relying on our eyes. Making it centered would be hard though. Yes, this is when you should use the *Alignment Tool*.

Before you can align your text, you need to select the whole text box with the alignment tool. Make sure the text layer is selected, then create a rectangle (exactly how you would work with the selection tools) around the text box.

Align to the center.

## This is how to do it

- **Tool Options Panel**:

You text should be aligned horizontally to the center now.

Printed in Great Britain
by Amazon